MAY 2 7 2022

A STRANGER WORLD

MOUNTAIN ATTACK

A YETI ENCOUNTER

BY ANITA CROY
ILLUSTRATED BY DIEGO VAISBERG

BEARPORT
PUBLISHING

Minneapolis, Minnesota

Credits: 20, © Daniel Eskridge/Shutterstock; 21t, © Daniel Eskridge/Shutterstock; 21c, © Linda Bucklin/Shutterstock; 21b, © szpeti/Shutterstock and © Linda Bucklin/Shutterstock; 22t, © Igor Shoshin/Shutterstock; 22b, © Tory Kallman/Shutterstock.

Editor: Sarah Eason
Proofreader: Harriet McGregor
Designers: Jessica Moon and Steve Mead
Picture Researcher: Rachel Blount

DISCLAIMER: This graphic story is a dramatization based on true events. It is intended to give the reader a sense of the narrative rather than a presentation of actual details as they occurred.

Library of Congress Cataloging-in-Publication Data

Names: Croy, Anita, author. | Vaisberg, Diego, illustrator.
Title: Mountain attack : a yeti encounter / by Anita Croy ; illustrated by Diego Vaisberg.
Description: Bear claw books edition. | Minneapolis, Minnesota : Bearport Publishing Company, [2022] | Series: A stranger world | Includes bibliographical references and index.
Identifiers: LCCN 2020058675 (print) | LCCN 2020058676 (ebook) | ISBN 9781636910079 (library binding) | ISBN 9781636910147 (paperback) | ISBN 9781636910215 (ebook)
Subjects: LCSH: Yeti--Himalaya Mountains--Juvenile literature. | Yeti--Himalaya Mountains--Comic books, strips, etc. | Graphic novels.
Classification: LCC QL89.2.Y4 C76 2022 (print) | LCC QL89.2.Y4 (ebook) | DDC 001.944095496--dc23
LC record available at https://lccn.loc.gov/2020058675
LC ebook record available at https://lccn.loc.gov/2020058676

Copyright © 2022 Bearport Publishing Company. All rights reserved. No part of this publication may be reproduced in whole or in part, stored in any retrieval system, or transmitted in any form or by any means, electronic, mechanical, photocopying, recording, or otherwise, without written permission from the publisher.

For more information, write to Bearport Publishing, 5357 Penn Avenue South, Minneapolis, MN 55419. Printed in the United States of America.

CONTENTS

Chapter 1
Mountain Mysteries 4

Chapter 2
Something Strange 6

Chapter 3
Mountain Rescue 12

Chapter 4
Lhakpa's Story 16

Monsters around the World 20
Fact or Fiction? 22
Glossary 23
Index 24
Read More 24
Learn More Online 24

CHAPTER 1

MOUNTAIN MYSTERIES

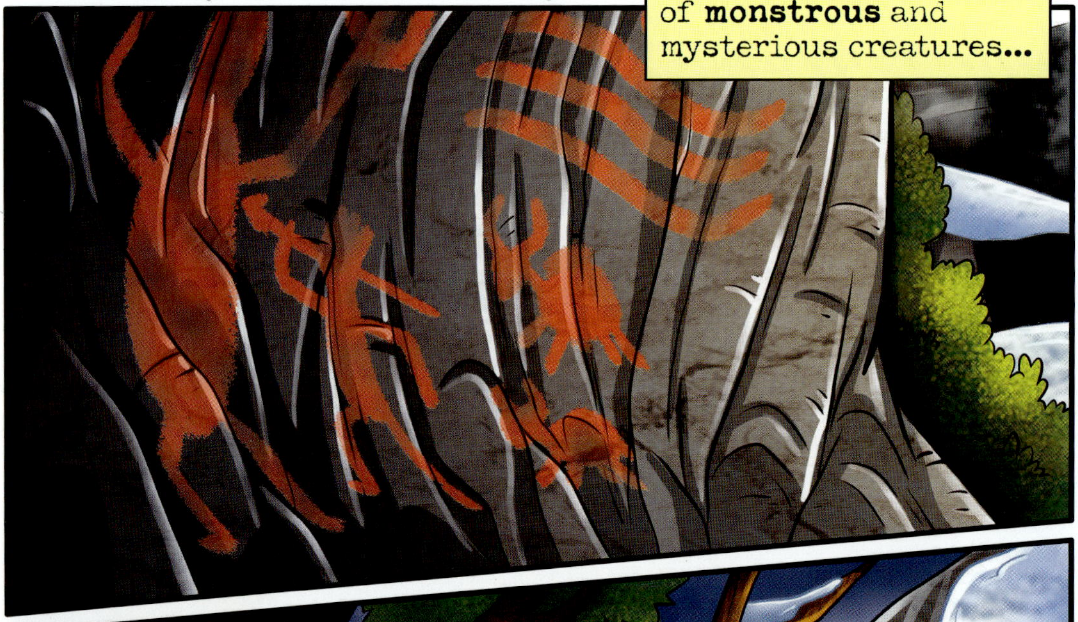
For years, people have told stories of **monstrous** and mysterious creatures...

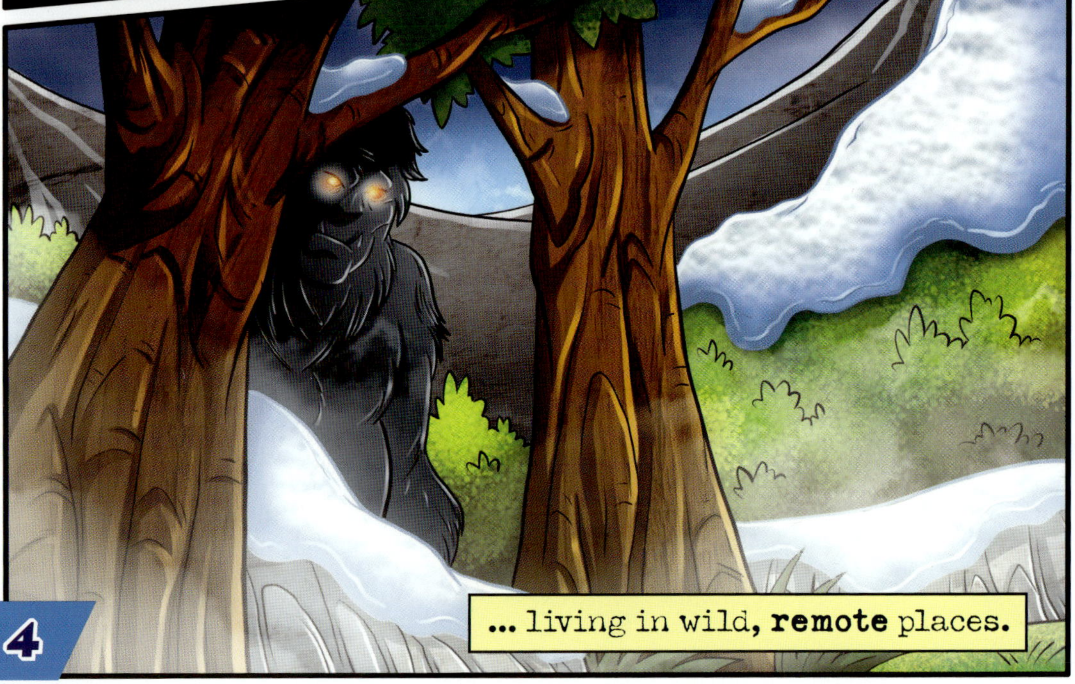
... living in wild, **remote** places.

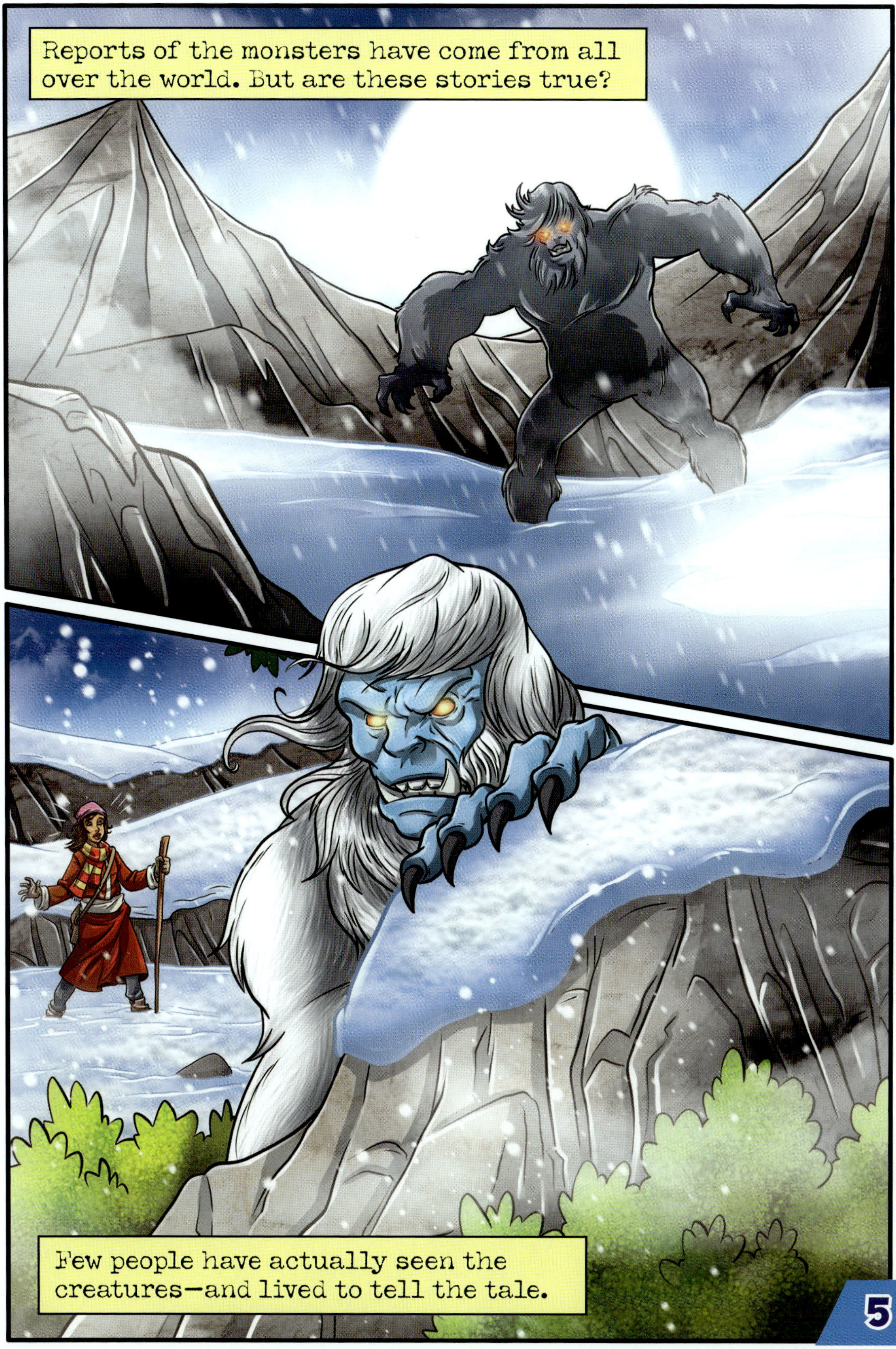
Reports of the monsters have come from all over the world. But are these stories true?
Few people have actually seen the creatures—and lived to tell the tale.

CHAPTER 2

SOMETHING STRANGE

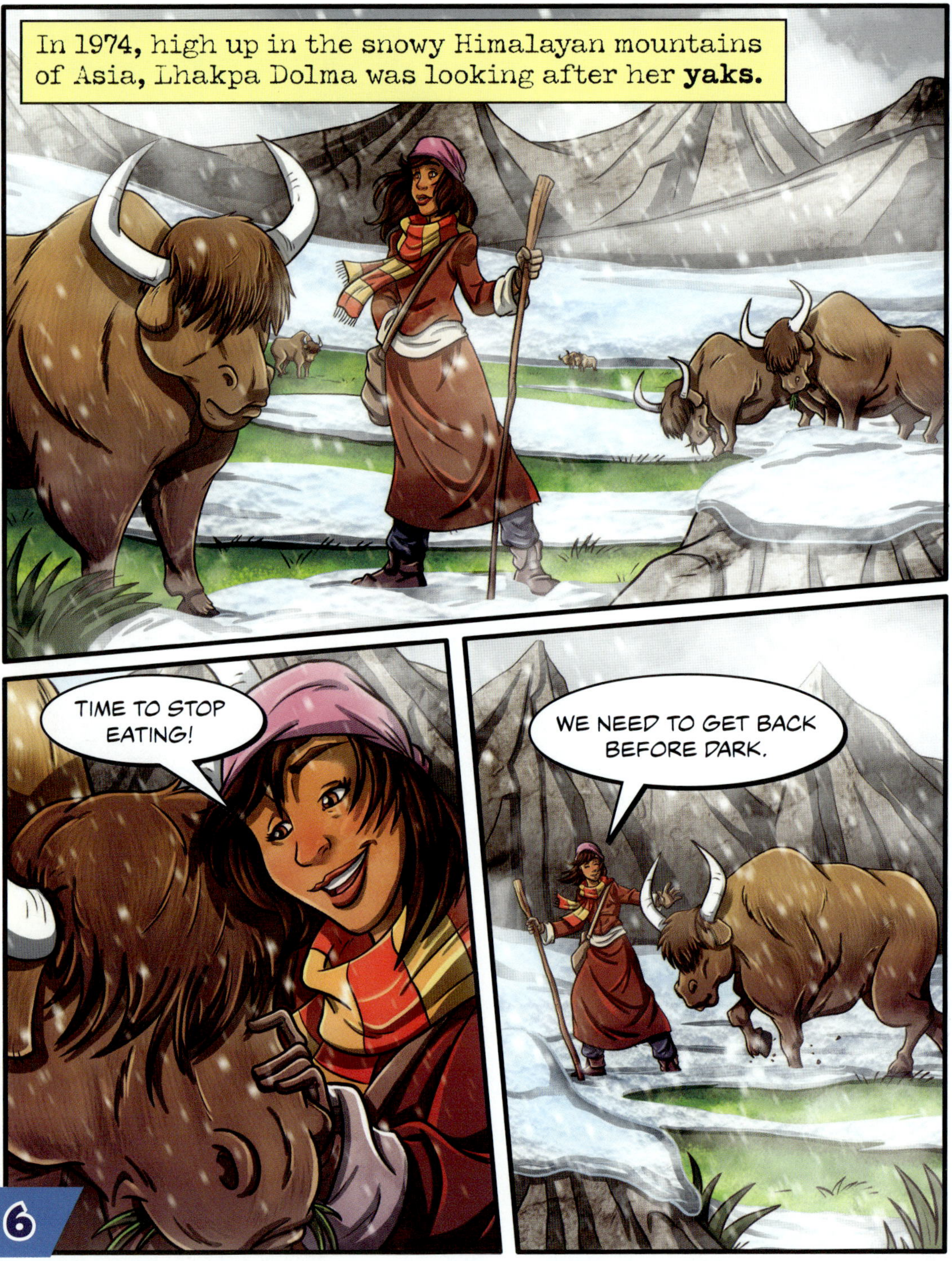
In 1974, high up in the snowy Himalayan mountains of Asia, Lhakpa Dolma was looking after her **yaks.**
TIME TO STOP EATING!
WE NEED TO GET BACK BEFORE DARK.

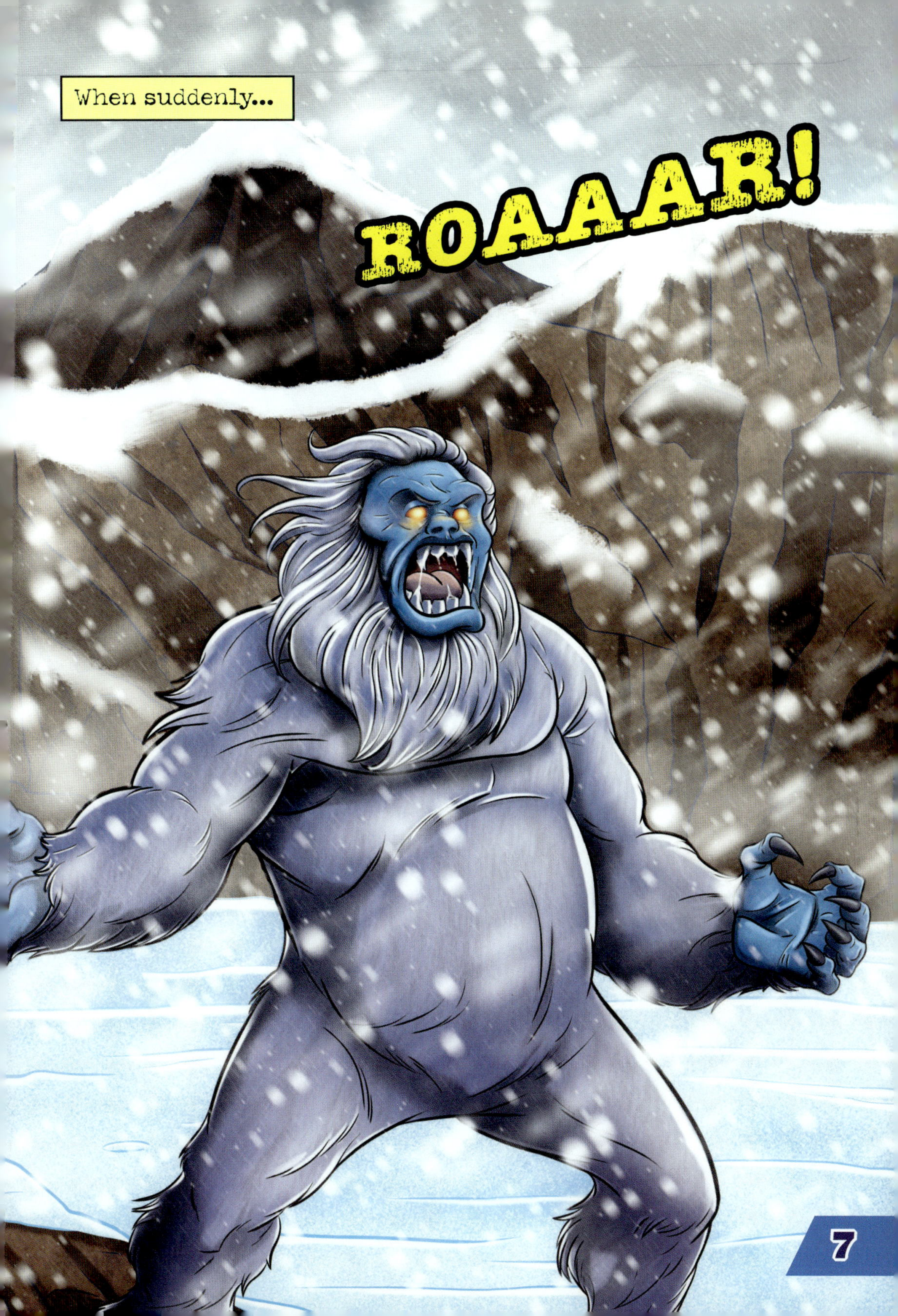
When suddenly...
ROAAAR!

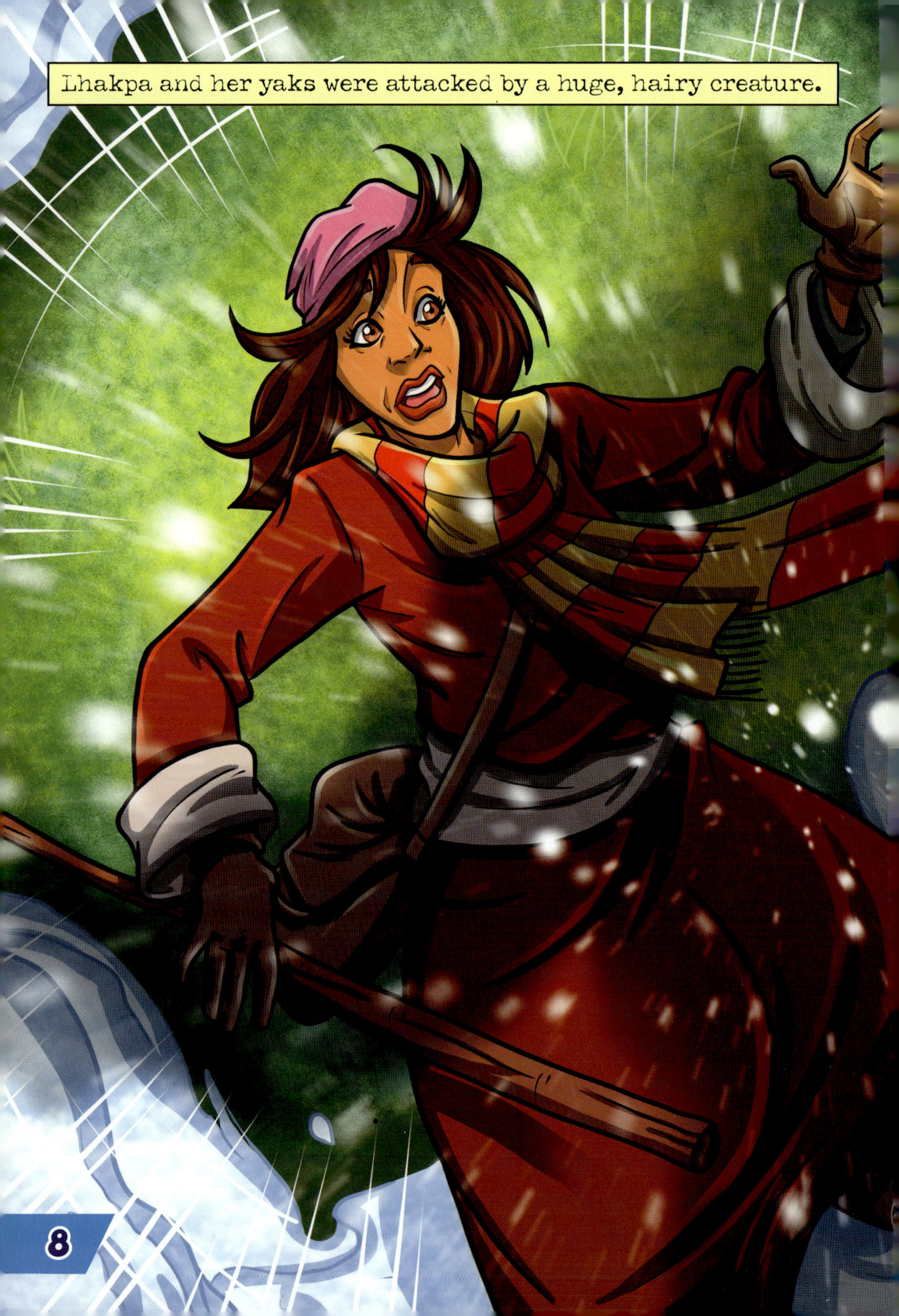
Lhakpa and her yaks were attacked by a huge, hairy creature.

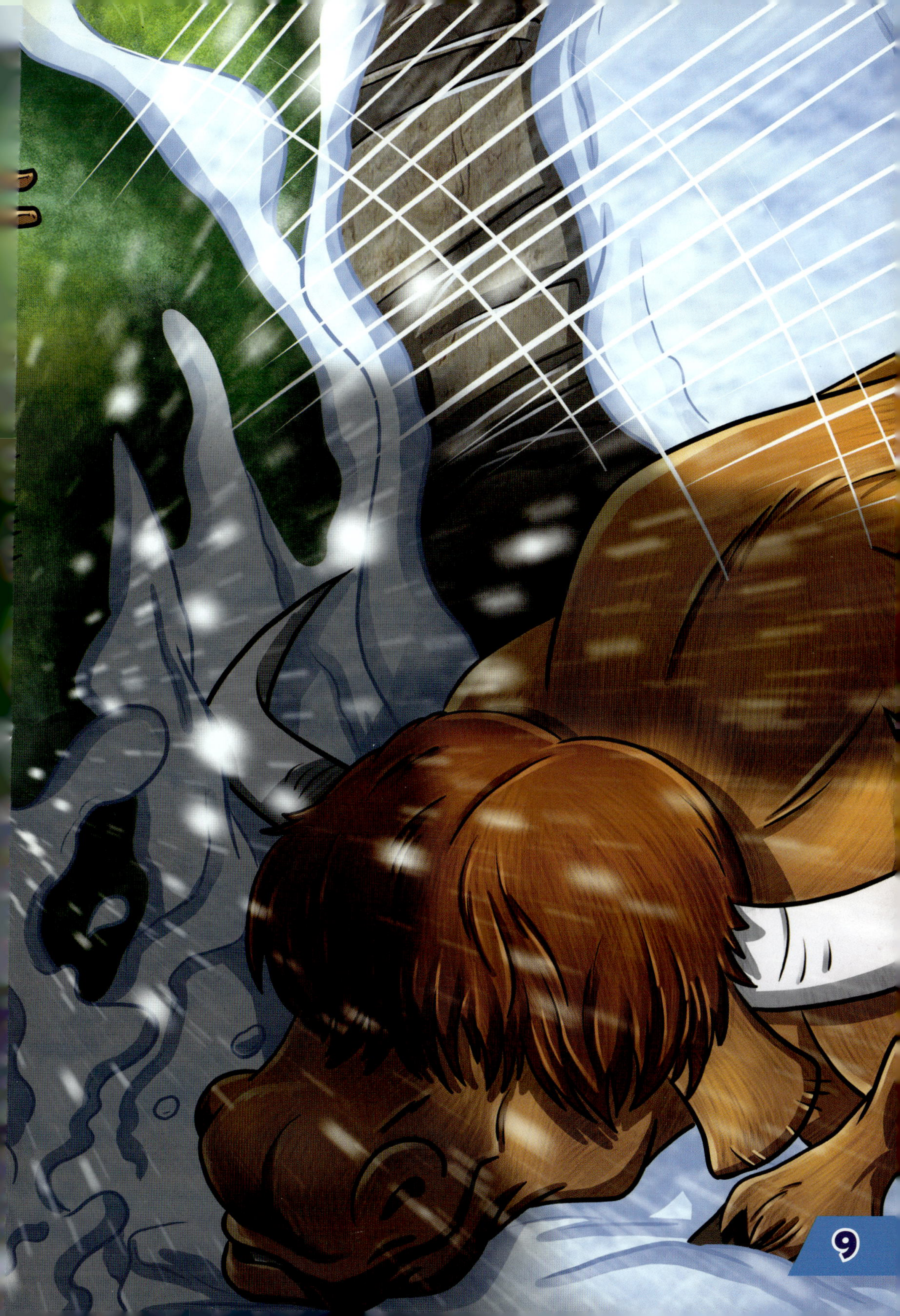

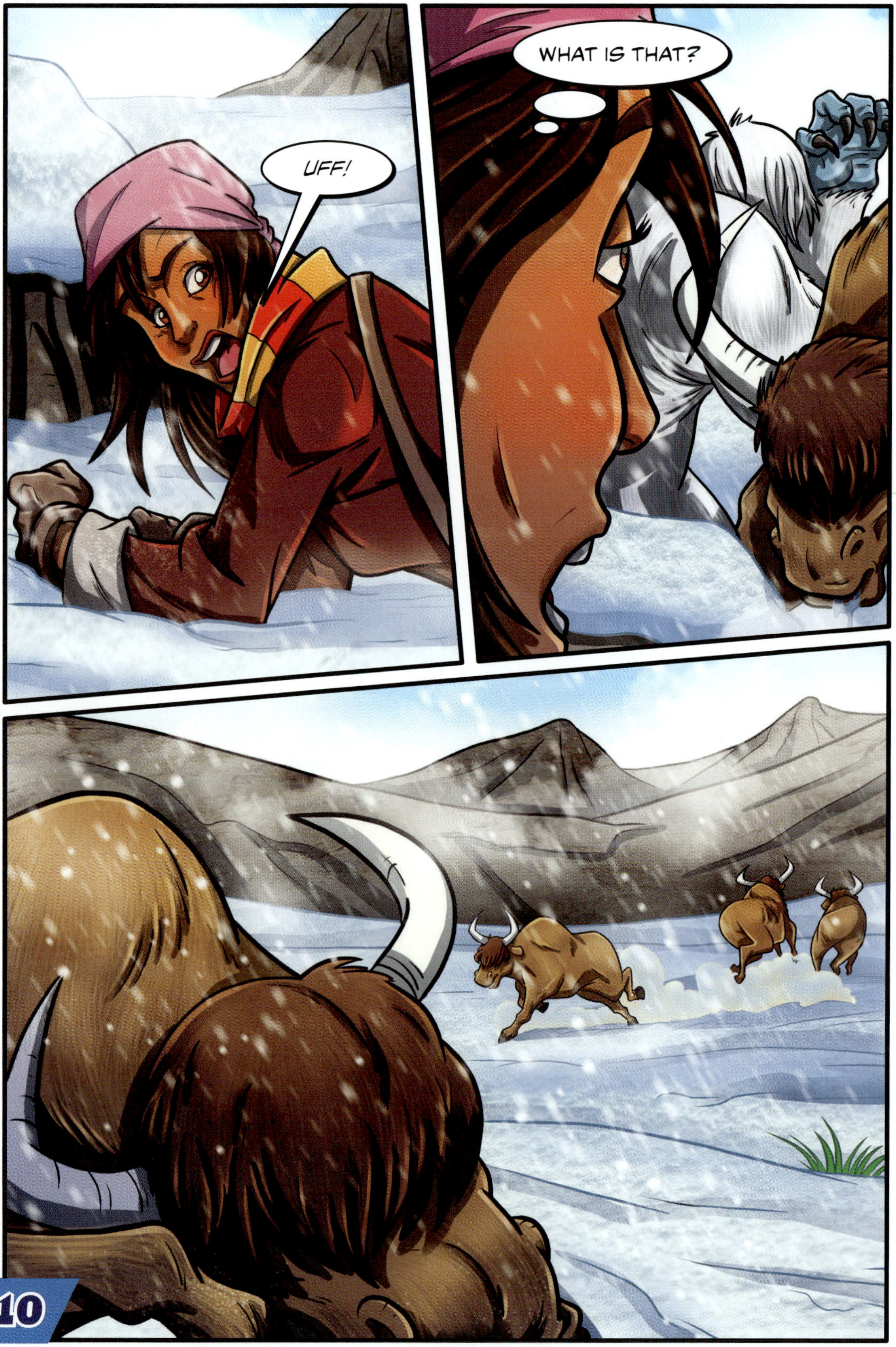
UFF!
WHAT IS THAT?

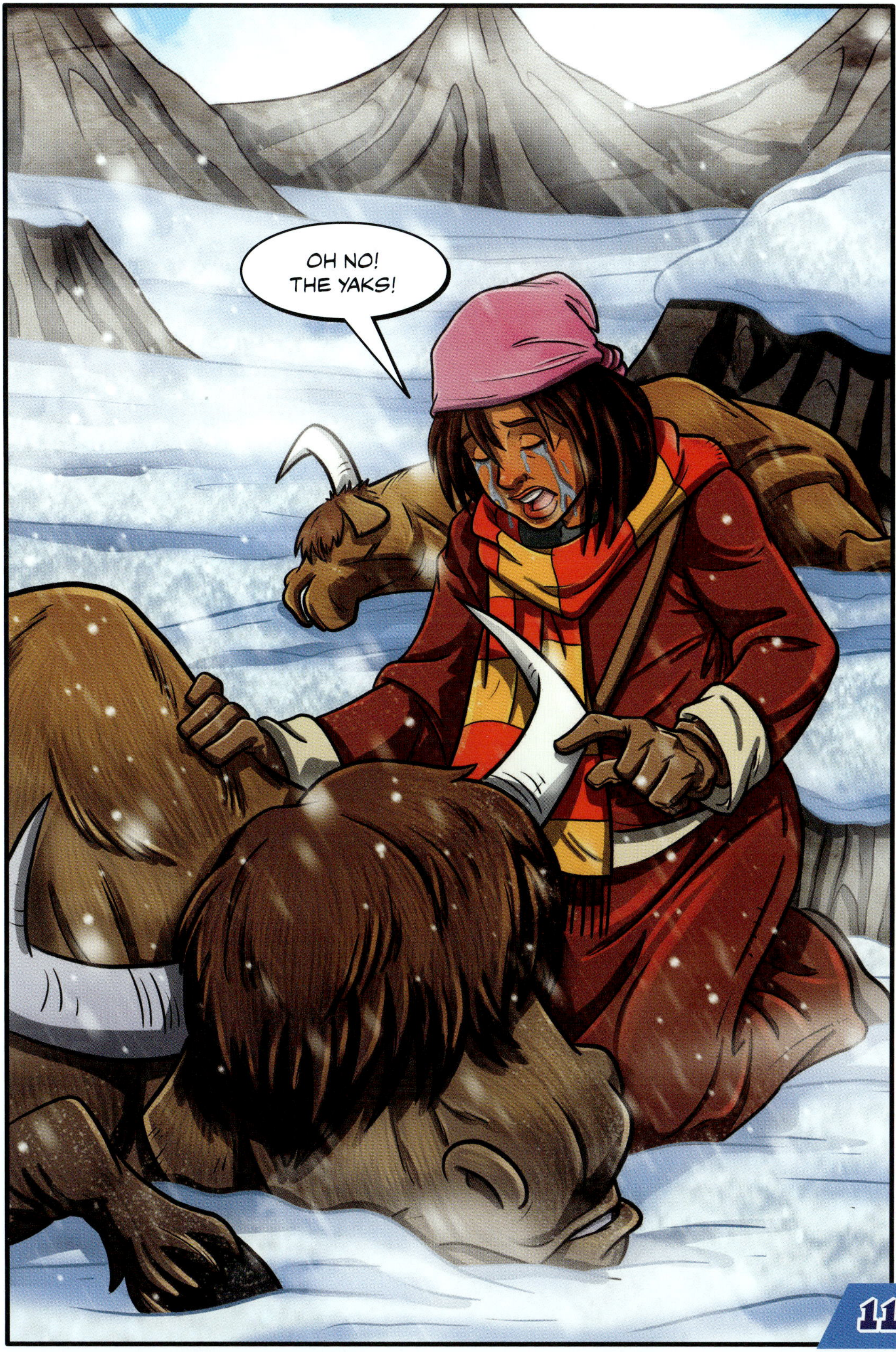
OH NO!
THE YAKS!

CHAPTER 3

MOUNTAIN RESCUE

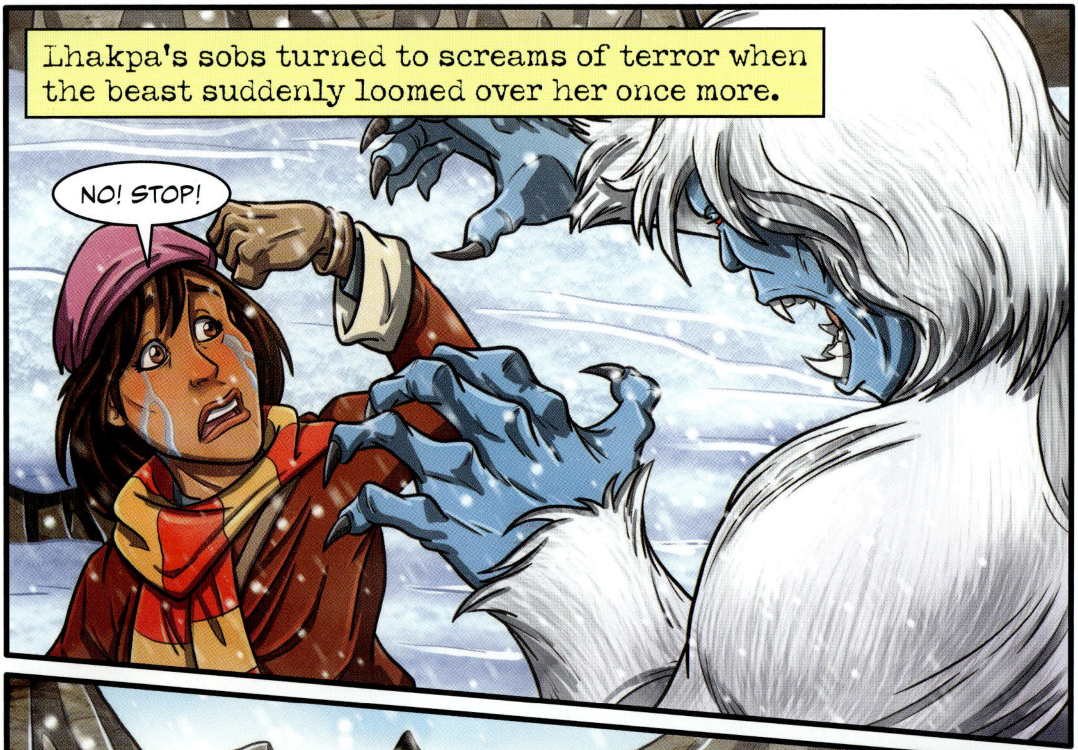
Lhakpa's sobs turned to screams of terror when the beast suddenly loomed over her once more.
NO! STOP!

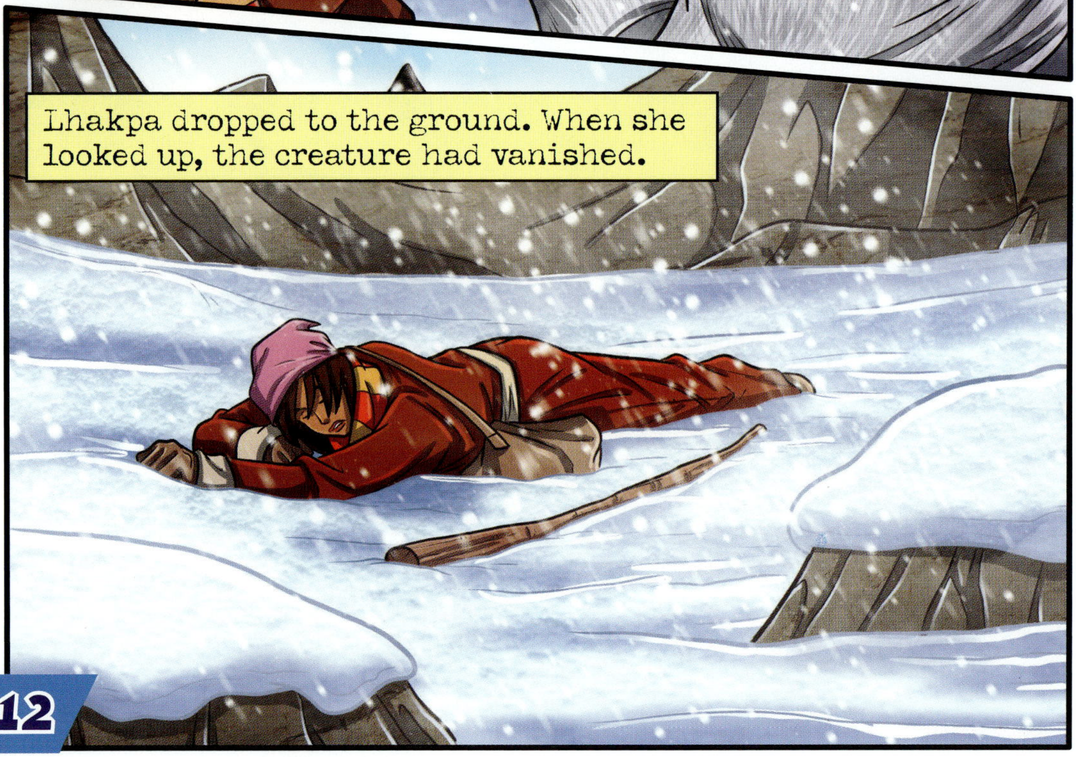
Lhakpa dropped to the ground. When she looked up, the creature had vanished.

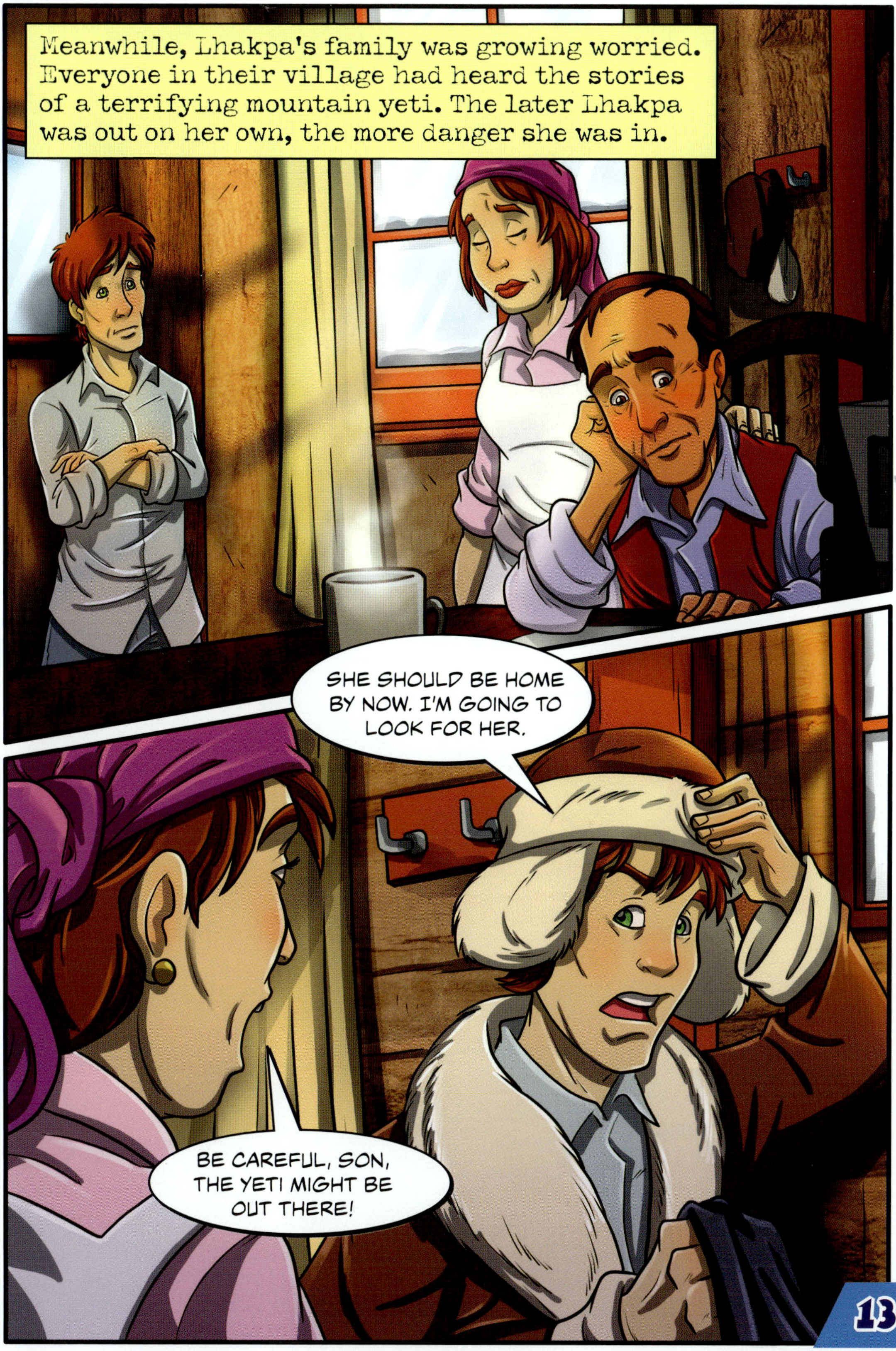
Meanwhile, Lhakpa's family was growing worried. Everyone in their village had heard the stories of a terrifying mountain yeti. The later Lhakpa was out on her own, the more danger she was in.
SHE SHOULD BE HOME BY NOW. I'M GOING TO LOOK FOR HER.
BE CAREFUL, SON, THE YETI MIGHT BE OUT THERE!

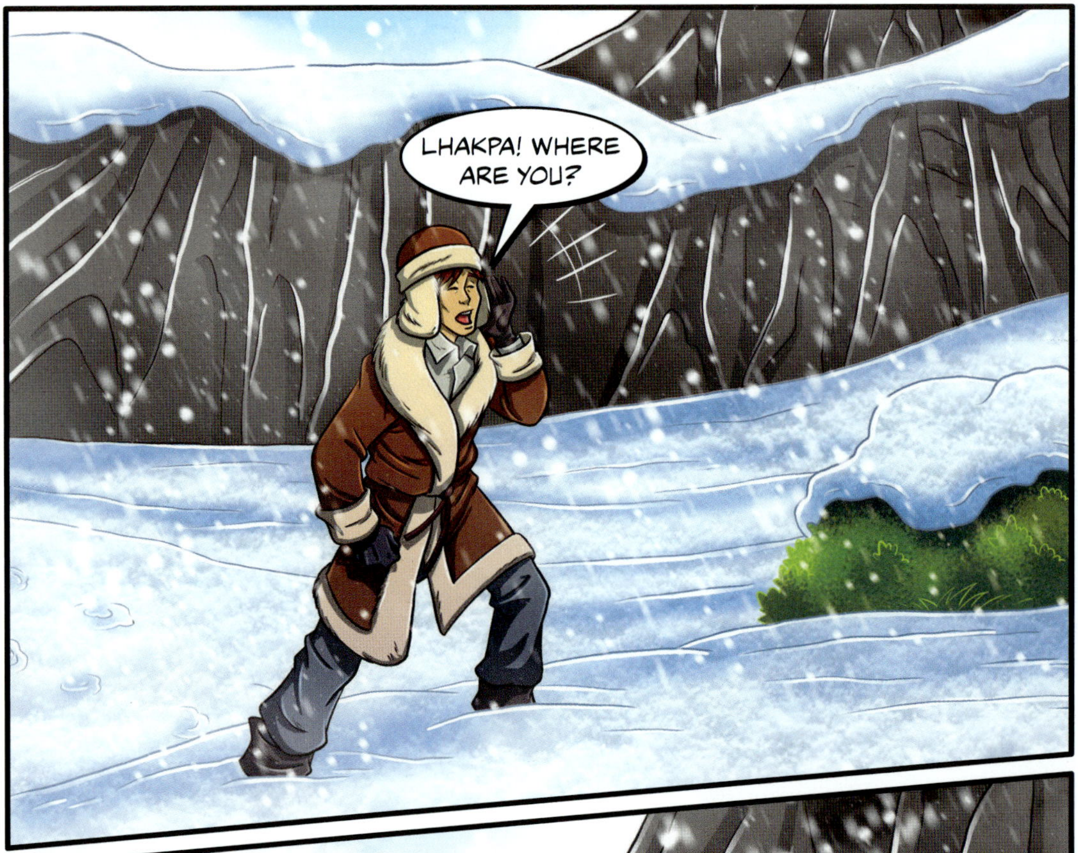
LHAKPA! WHERE ARE YOU?

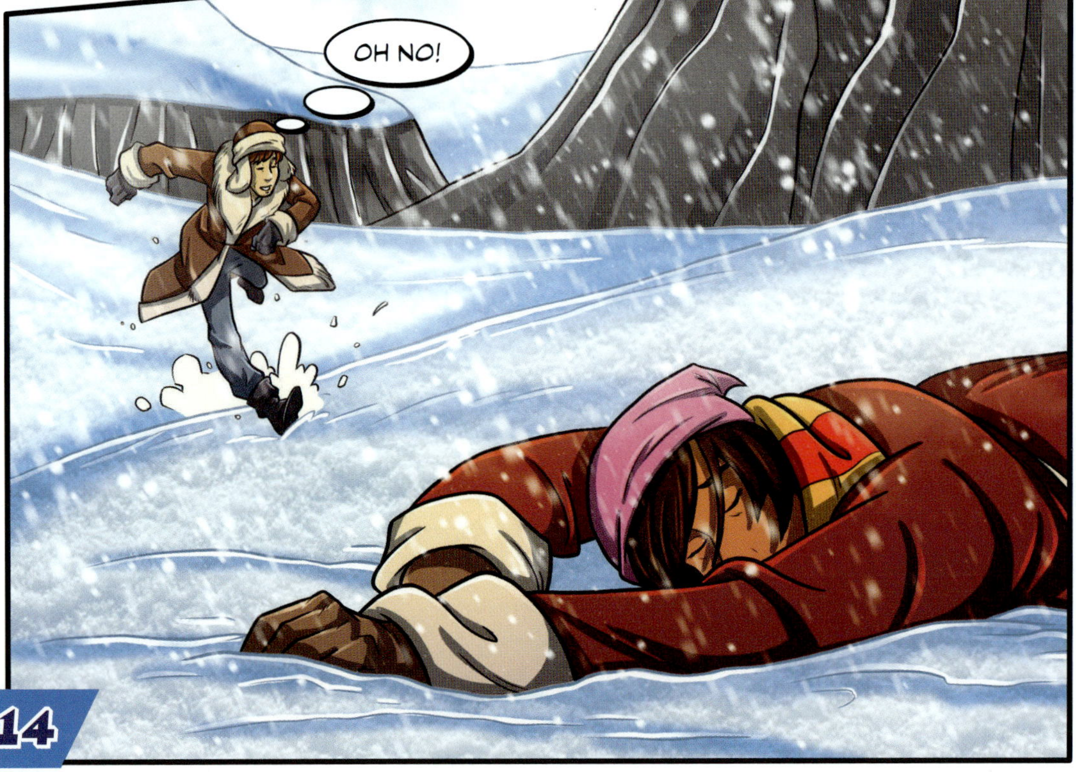
OH NO!

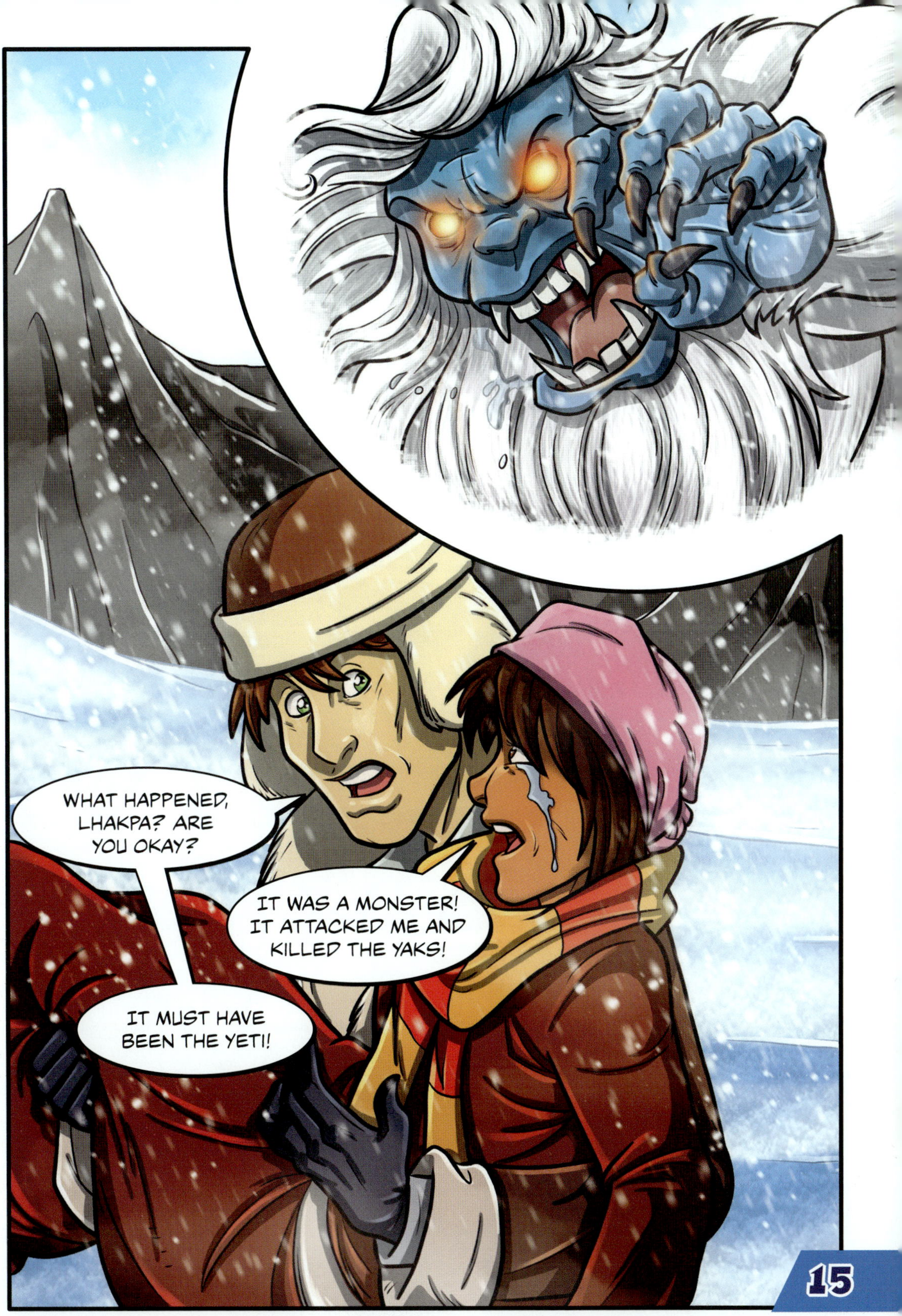
WHAT HAPPENED, LHAKPA? ARE YOU OKAY?
IT WAS A MONSTER! IT ATTACKED ME AND KILLED THE YAKS!
IT MUST HAVE BEEN THE YETI!

CHAPTER 4

LHAKPA'S STORY

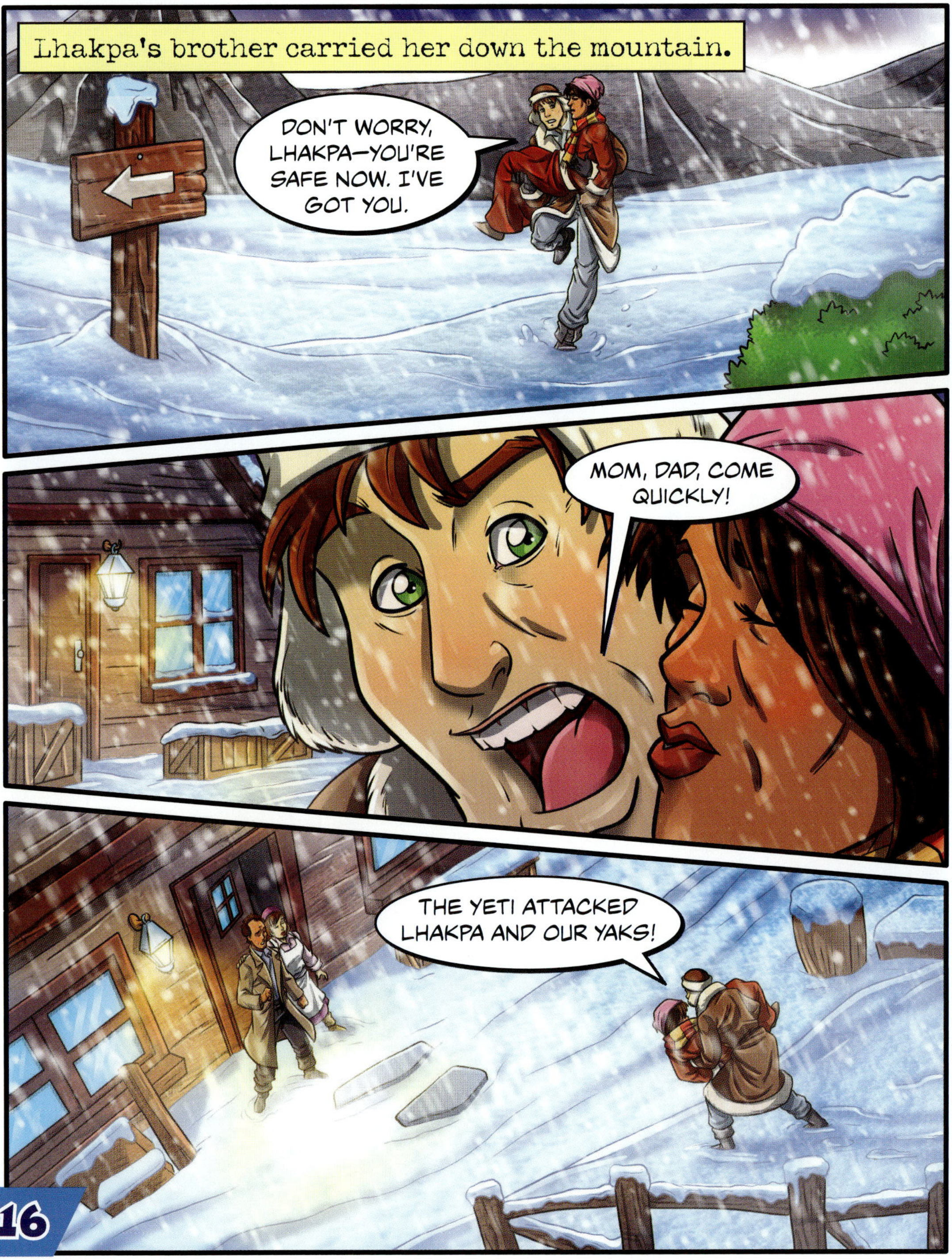
Lhakpa's brother carried her down the mountain.
DON'T WORRY, LHAKPA—YOU'RE SAFE NOW. I'VE GOT YOU.
MOM, DAD, COME QUICKLY!
THE YETI ATTACKED LHAKPA AND OUR YAKS!

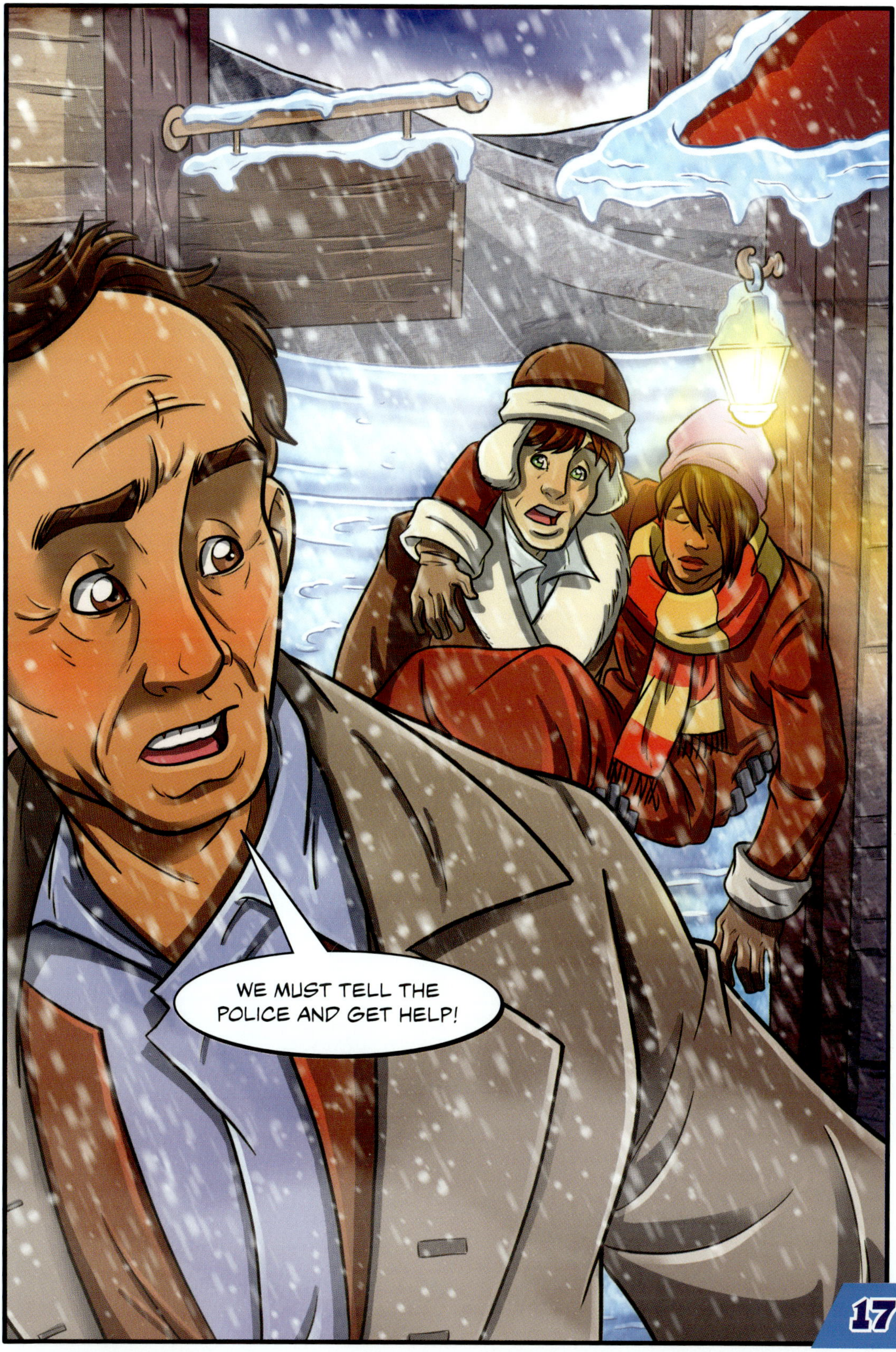
WE MUST TELL THE POLICE AND GET HELP!

The police officer listened to Lhakpa's **description** of the beast.

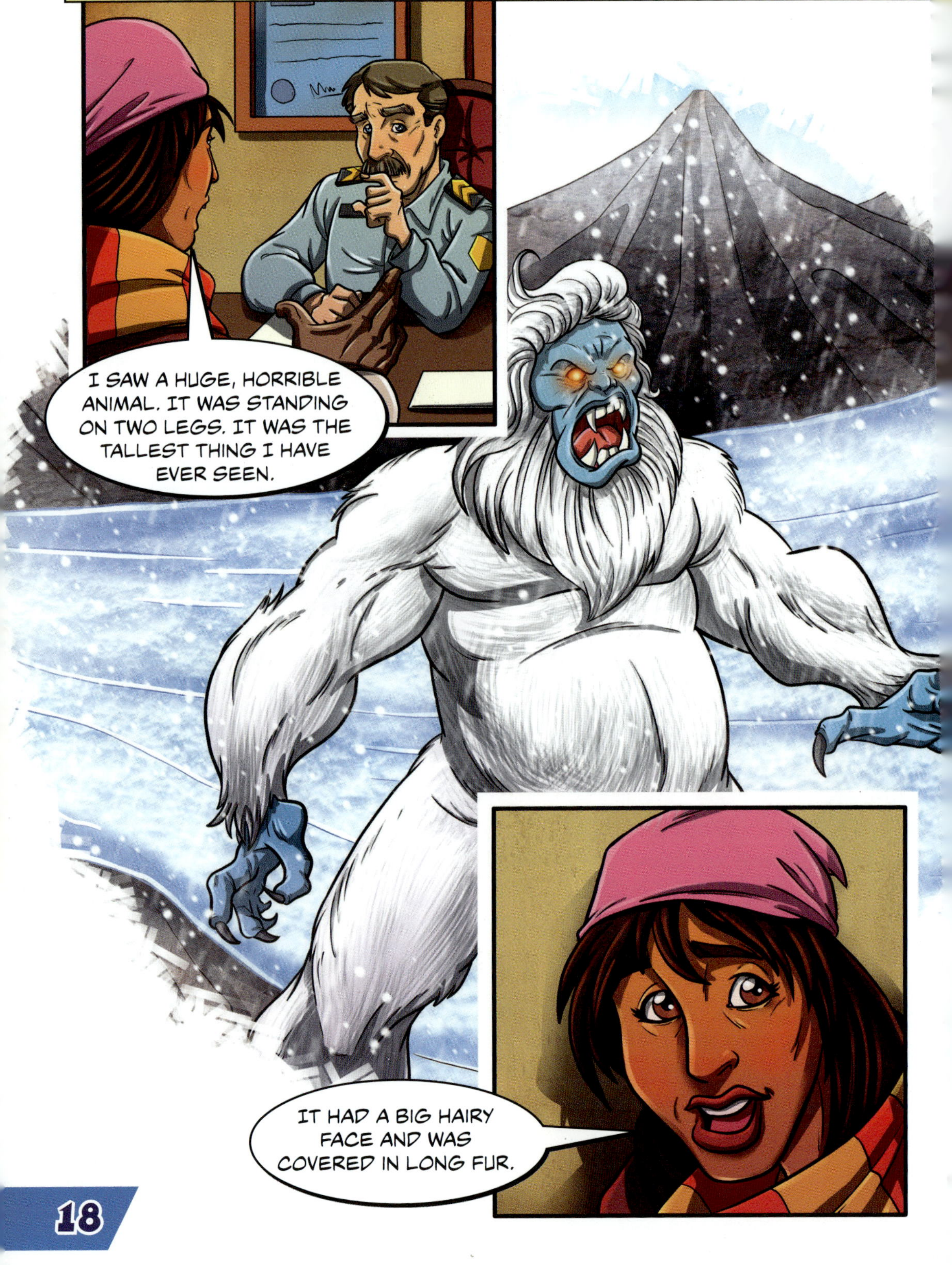
I SAW A HUGE, HORRIBLE ANIMAL. IT WAS STANDING ON TWO LEGS. IT WAS THE TALLEST THING I HAVE EVER SEEN.
IT HAD A BIG HAIRY FACE AND WAS COVERED IN LONG FUR.

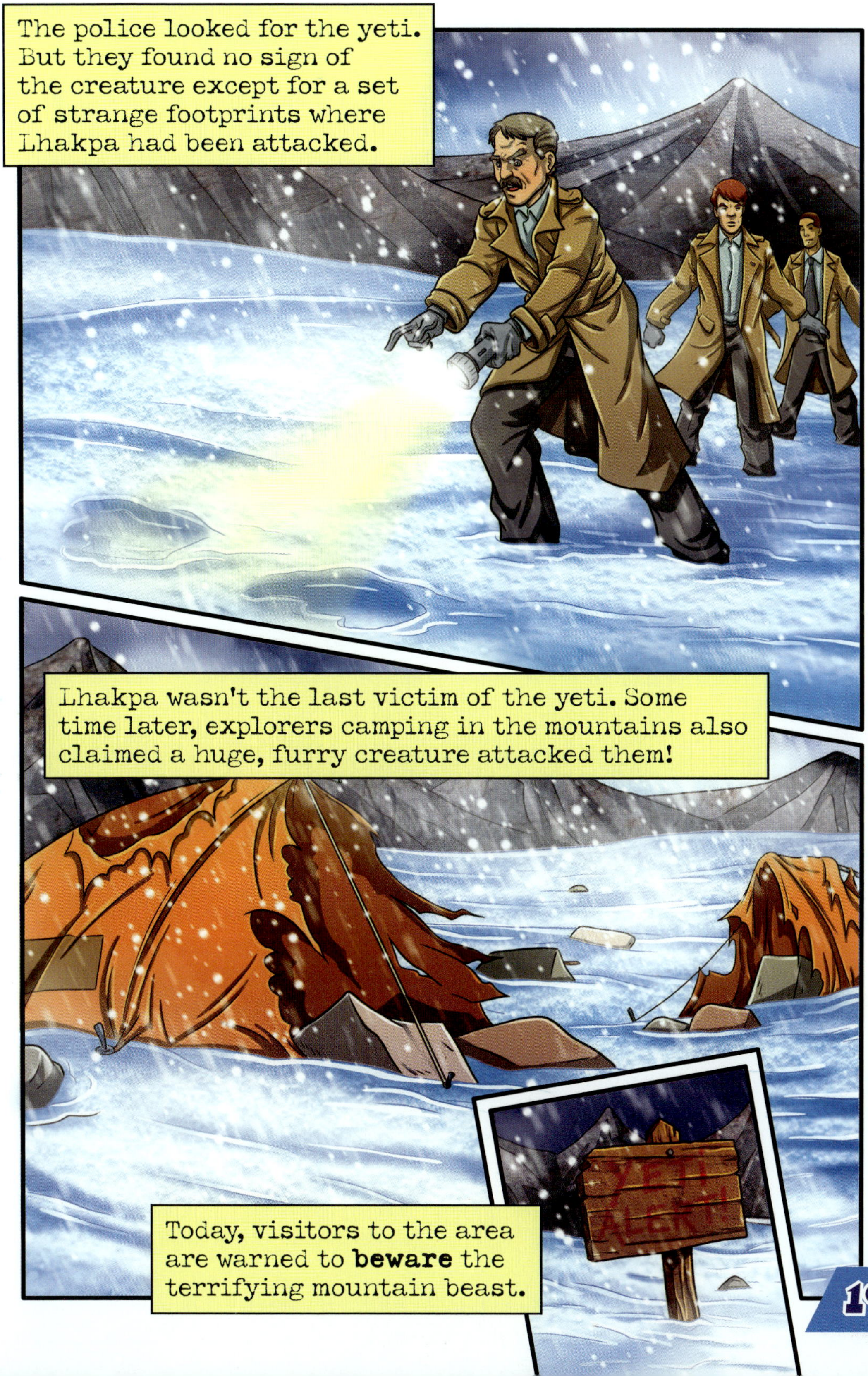
The police looked for the yeti. But they found no sign of the creature except for a set of strange footprints where Lhakpa had been attacked.
Lhakpa wasn't the last victim of the yeti. Some time later, explorers camping in the mountains also claimed a huge, furry creature attacked them!
YETI ALERT!
Today, visitors to the area are warned to **beware** the terrifying mountain beast.

MONSTERS AROUND THE WORLD

Stories of monster-like creatures have long been told around the world. Learn all about some of world's most terrifying creatures.

THE LOCH NESS MONSTER (NESSIE)

LIVES: IN LOCH NESS, A LAKE IN SCOTLAND

DESCRIPTION: A 30-FOOT (9 M) SEA SERPENT WITH A LONG NECK AND A TINY HEAD

MONSTER BEHAVIOR: THE LOCH NESS MONSTER SPENDS MOST OF ITS TIME AT THE BOTTOM OF THE DEEP LAKE. ITS NECK AND HEAD OCCASIONALLY POP UP OUT OF THE WATER. NESSIE HUNTERS HAVE TRIED TO CAPTURE THE MONSTER FOR YEARS, BUT IT ALWAYS **EVADES** THEM.

YOWIE

LIVES: IN THE AUSTALIAN FORESTS

DESCRIPTION: AN APELIKE CREATURE THAT WALKS ON TWO FEET. IT STANDS BETWEEN 5 AND 10 FT (1.5–3 M) TALL AND SMELLS LIKE PEE, POOP, AND ROTTEN EGGS.

MONSTER BEHAVIOR: THE YOWIE HIDES IN THICK FOREST AND COMES OUT AT NIGHT TO WATCH CAMPERS.

MOKELE-MBEMBE

LIVES: IN THE RIVERS AND LAKES OF AFRICA

DESCRIPTION: A DINOSAUR-LIKE MONSTER THAT WALKS ON FOUR FEET. IT CAN GROW TO 75 FT (23 M) LONG.

MONSTER BEHAVIOR: IT SPENDS MOST OF ITS TIME IN WATER AND SOMETIMES TIPS OVER BOATS, KILLING THE PEOPLE ON BOARD.

THUNDERBIRD

LIVES: IN NORTH AMERICA

DESCRIPTION: A HUGE BIRD WITH AN ENORMOUS **WINGSPAN** AS BIG AS A SMALL PLANE.

MONSTER BEHAVIOR: ON JULY 25, 1977, TWO MONSTER BIRDS FLEW INTO 10-YEAR-OLD MARLON LOWE'S BACKYARD IN LAWNDALE, ILLINOIS. ONE MONSTER GRABBED MARLON'S SHOULDERS AND LIFTED HIM OFF THE GROUND. LUCKILY, THE MONSTER DROPPED THE BOY BEFORE IT FLEW OFF.

FACT OR FICTION?

Scientists and **eyewitnesses** have argued for years about whether the yeti and other related monsters—such as its North American cousin, Bigfoot—really exist.

Some people claim to have photographic **proof** of a large, hairy monster that lurks in forests. Other people think that Bigfoot is just a very big brown bear. Still others wonder if Bigfoot and the yeti could be the **descendants** of a **prehistoric** ape.

STORIES ABOUT BIGFOOT BEGAN IN THE 1950S, WHEN PEOPLE DISCOVERED GIANT FOOTPRINTS IN THE FOREST.

In Puerto Rico, people talk of a similar monster known as the chupacabra, or goat sucker, that kills **livestock**. In 1995, it killed eight sheep and drank all the blood in their bodies. People describe the beast as a large, hairless dog with scaly skin. However, coyotes sometimes get a skin disease called mange that causes them to lose all their hair. Could the chupacabra be just a sick coyote?

COULD PEOPLE HAVE MISTAKEN A SICK COYOTE FOR A MONSTER?

GLOSSARY

beware to be careful

descendants the children or offspring of someone or something

description a spoken or written account of an object, person, or place

evades gets away using special skills

eyewitnesses people who see or hear something taking place

livestock animals, such as sheep, that are raised by people on farms or ranches

monstrous something that looks like a monster

prehistoric belonging to a time before written history

proof anything that shows something is real

remote a place that is far away with few or no people living there

wingspan the distance from the tip of one wing to the tip of the other wing

yaks large oxen with long hair and long, curved horns

INDEX

Asia 6
attack 8, 15-16, 19
Bigfoot 22
Himalayan mountains 6
Loch Ness Monster 20
Mokele-Mbembe 21

mountains 4, 6, 12-13, 16, 19
police 17-19
Thunderbird 21
yaks 6, 8, 11, 15-16
yeti 13, 15-16, 19, 22
Yowie 21

READ MORE

Borgert-Spaniol, Megan. *Cryptozoology: Could Unexplained Creatures Be Real? (Science Fact or Science Fiction?).* Minneapolis: Abdo Publishing, 2019.

Cole, Bradley. *Bigfoot (Monster Histories).* North Mankato, MN: Capstone Press, 2020.

Gish, Ashley. *Bigfoot (X-Books: Mythical Creatures).* Mankato, MN: Creative Education, 2019.

LEARN MORE ONLINE

1. Go to **www.factsurfer.com**
2. Enter **"Mountain Attack"** into the search box.
3. Click on the cover of this book to see a list of websites.